Simple
Welcome
Speeches

Amy Bolding

SIMPLE
WELCOME
SPEECHES
AND OTHER HELPS

SIMPLE WELCOME SPEECHES
AND OTHER HELPS

Amy Bolding

Introductions
Replies
Thanks
Welcomes

BAKER BOOK HOUSE
Grand Rapids, Michigan

ISBN:0-8010-0612-0

Eighteenth printing, December 1996

Fomerly published under the title:
Handy Introductions and Replies

Printed in the United States of America

Contents

This book is dedicated with love and respect to my friend, Mrs. A. C. (Eloise) Drake. Her devotion to duty has been an example to all her friends.

Introductions

... For Ministers

A star has arisen on the spiritual horizon of our state. His beams of pristine glory and power will fall upon many before his ministry is finished. He is a minister called of God. He has many talents but he has chosen to use them for the glory of the Lord. I am speaking to you about our speaker for this hour, Mr. _____.

★　★　★

Once in a generation a man is called of God to stand out above others as a great leader and preacher. Such a man is our speaker for today. He has celestial power from on high. He urges the people to repent and turn to faith in Jesus, our Lord. We are indeed fortunate that he could take time from a very busy schedule and come to bring our message today.

★　★　★

Not since the days of William Jennings Bryan has a popular public speaker received the resounding acclaim and praise that has befallen our speaker for today. He is the pastor of a large church yet he finds time to answer the demands of the people ever to go afield and speak in the name of our Lord Jesus Christ. He is so popular as a speaker there are times when his wife asks for an audience so she can talk to him for brief periods. Seriously, we are blessed to have Bro. _____ today and will hear him gladly.

★　★　★

Our speaker for today is Mr. _____. He is pastor of the church in _____. We feel he will bless us greatly as he speaks from many years of experience and background as a pastor. People who belong to his church tell me he never speaks without inspiring them to work harder for the cause of Christ. We are so glad to have this great and good man in our own church today.

★ ★ ★

As I have had the privilege to listen to Dr. _____ from time to time I have asked myself, "How does he do it?"

He carries on as a pastor, as worker in civic projects in his city, as a husband and father, and does a great deal of counseling work.

Today he will speak to us on a subject very close to his heart, a subject to which he has given much time and thought. I recommend that we listen with attention as we hear this dynamic man.

★ ★ ★

I count it an honor to be asked to introduce our speaker for today. He is one of the most gifted speakers I have ever known. After you hear him I believe you will resolve to live more effectively for the Lord about whom he comes to tell us.

★ ★ ★

As I arranged my thoughts regarding our speaker of the hour, I realized what an influence he has had on my own life. He is the type of man who never speaks unless he has something to say. He has something to say so people like to listen to him. We anticipate a great time together. He is a busy pastor. He ranks especially high in the eyes of his fellow townsmen, having been pastor in the city of _____ for a number of years. We count it a blessing that you came our way today.

★ ★ ★

Time will not permit me to give you a biographical sketch of our speaker's life. Believe me, it has been a colorful life and a useful one. In this unusual man we find one who lives daily what he preaches constantly. The hour is never too late for him to go to the aid of someone in distress. He

10

is a powerful force against evil in his city and I know as we listen we will see the immense importance of the work he represents.

★   ★   ★

Someone has said: "Americans listen very little." I believe I am about to introduce to you one who will grip your heart and make you listen to his message.

Bro. _____ is an enthusiastic person. He keeps a very aggressive and active program going in the city where he is pastor.

★   ★   ★

Bro. _____ is a scholarly gentleman from our neighboring town of _____. He speaks with candor and a wide knowledge of world affairs today. He has made a study of the world situation during these times of doubt and controversy. He has often turned the weapons of scholarship against the forces of evil in his community. We are so glad to have Bro. _____ as our speaker today.

★   ★   ★

For many years I have counted Bro. _____ as one of my dearest friends. It is a joy for me to be able to introduce him today. You will find him to be entirely orthodox. I have been privileged to hear Bro. _____ on many occasions and always I found him to be tremendously interesting and inspiring.

★   ★   ★

Our speaker today is one who has a tremendous insight into the teachings of Jesus. He has helped many to gain a greater understanding of the Scriptures. In our denomination he is outstanding as a student of the Bible. He has inspired others to study more and gain greater knowledge.

★   ★   ★

A rich spiritual experience is in store for you as you hear this wonderful man of God preach to us today. He has won many souls to a saving knowledge of Jesus Christ. I count it a red-letter day for us to have him preach today.

★ ★ ★

Our minister today is one who at times preaches some severe sermons. I feel sure it is fine for him to preach on the sins of the people down the street, or even next door but when he gets to my sins I want to tune him off. Now today I feel sure he will step on all our toes and try his best to put us to work. Well, maybe we should listen and go to work. Seriously, I think he is a great preacher and a fearless one. We are glad to have you.

★ ★ ★

As our speaker comes to bring us a message, will you be earnestly in prayer that significant and right decisions will be made in this service?

Bro. _____ is an ordinary man who, in the providence of God, has lived an extraordinary life. He has been pastor in some cities where turbulent happenings have called for a very strong Christian witness. We are fortunate to be able to hear his experiences today.

★ ★ ★

We come to hear one tonight who for a number of years has preached the word of God fearlessly and dynamically. Bro. _____ has a great love for people. The main objective of his life has been "people." His church has grown tremendously in the years he has been pastor. Many who have known him through the years will say: "I thank my God upon every rememberance of you."

... For Evangelists

We have been looking forward to the arrival of our evangelist. He has preached in many evangelistic meetings, resulting, by the mercy of God, in the salvation of many.

His simple messages are to present to lost men the triumphant and saving gospel of Jesus Christ. We will back him with our prayers during this series of services.

★   ★   ★

It is with the deepest prayer in my heart that I present to you our evangelist today. My hope is that many will find inspiration and courage to go out and bring the lost to our services. Our evangelist is a man who exhorts and appeals to men that they might seek and find trust in Christ. He comes to us highly recommended by other pastors who have used his services. We will look forward to a great spiritual awakening.

★   ★   ★

The hearts of Christian people have been thrilled in many places by our evangelist. We are indeed fortunate to be able to secure his services for this series of meetings. He has the gift of preaching. The Holy Spirit has anointed him with power. God has blessed us by sending him our way. Now we must get under the burden of prayer for the lost and bring them to hear this mighty man of God.

★   ★   ★

Our revival starts today under the leadership of a great evangelist. He is one of America's finest young preachers. He has had great success in leading young people. Wherever he has led a revival campaign, the attendance has been outstanding. God has opened many doors for him that seemed hopelessly closed. He is not only a brilliant young preacher but he is a man of prayer.

13

We must expect great things these next few days and work to make them come to pass.

★　★　★

Our evangelist is a graduate of _____ school. He is married and the father of _____ children. His busy schedule keeps him away from home a great deal but his family is sympathetic with his work.

His ministry has been effective with young people and adults alike. Over and over I have heard him say that he attributes his success as an evangelist solely to God and His grace.

★　★　★

Our evangelist is a man with a voice like that of John the Baptist. He urges the people to turn from their wicked ways and repent. If you do not want to hear sin preached against this week you might best stay at home. This man of God preaches as he feels God would have him do. He daily increases in power as he works to bring in the kingdom.

★　★　★

Our evangelist is a man determined to do the work of God in the place to which he feels God has called him. It was not easy for him to resign a good church where he had been pastor for some time and go into the work of evangelism. His conviction that it was God's will, helped overcome the difficulties of travel and often being away from his dear family.

Before becoming a full time evangelist he was pastor of the church in _____. He holds a degree from _____ College. We will cooperate in every way possible to make his stay in our city a profitable one for our church.

★　★　★

We have a gifted man with us for this series of services. He did not bring a revival in his pocket. He will preach his heart out but we must also remember the admonition: "Let no man so envy his fellow's gift as to neglect his own; but let each one do what he can, and look to God for a blessing."

★ ★ ★

We expect this week to feast on spiritual food brought to us in a new and delightful way by our visiting evangelist. He will preach to us the old, old story in a new way. I am most happy to have him with us. As he asks us to participate in different ways let us remember, "The night cometh when no man can work." It becomes us to be diligent in the service of our Lord.

★ ★ ★

I want to present to you a man who seeks the will of the Spirit of God. He has been blessed as few men have in his ministry. He gives all the credit to our Heavenly Father. His messages will appeal to both believers and the unsaved. Here is a man who posseses honesty of heart and uprightness before God. Our committee selected him after much prayer and seeking after God's will. We will have a great time together.

★ ★ ★

The more I know the man I come to introduce to you, the more fascinated I become with his ministry. His treasure house of illustrations is inexhaustible. You will find each sermon new and exciting. We count the Lord has sent us a very desirable man for our revival. His helpful influence will live on long after he has left our city. I present him to you with the very highest recommendation.

★ ★ ★

I am deeply concerned that we have spiritual fellowship and unity with this fine man who comes to preach for us. He sometimes uses a new and different approach but always his emphasis is on the need of the lost world for a living Saviour. Whatever I may say about this good man will not adequately prepare you for the spiritual blessings in store for his listeners this week.

★ ★ ★

Our evangelist has come to us from a large and busy pastorate. His one aim in coming for these services is to help us all to know the wondrous story of Jesus, and to help us live it and tell it so as to win others to Christ.

Bro. ＿＿＿＿＿＿ is a well-known preacher in our denomination. He has led in many of the forward movements of our day. In spite of the many honors he has received he remains a humble servant of God, ever willing to serve when called.

* * *

Our evangelist is well known over our state. He preaches in the language of the people. He places great stress upon the Bible and its teachings. Bro. ＿＿＿＿＿＿ is as familiar with the teachings of the Bible as any minister alive today. He will bring to us new assurances of salvation and security. I assure you that if you attend all the services during this revival, at the close you will be able to give a reason for the faith that is in you.

* * *

Our visitor is truly a man who has proved worthy of the trust which he has from God. He has been found faithful through many years of work for the Lord. I hope each of you will co-operate fully as he seeks to lead us in an effort to reach every unsaved and unenlisted person in our town.

* * *

Bro. ＿＿＿＿＿＿ loves our city and our church. He knows both well, having grown up here. He also knows our possibilities. He is here to give of his time to help us reach our highest development. He is one of the strongest evangelists in our denomination today. Come to the services and feel the excitement.

* * *

Bro. ＿＿＿＿＿＿ has handed me a list of the most exciting subjects on which he will be preaching during this series of services. He has led a gripping and romantic life. He is one of the most picturesque men in the ministry today. He comes

16

from pioneer rural ancestry. I doubt if he is surpassed as an evangelist by any living man in our denomination today.

★   ★   ★

The one I am going to present to you now goes by a name recognized in church circles the country over. He is an evangelist of remarkable power. He has been actively engaged in evangelistic work for _____ years. He was "raised" in the country, educated in town and will preach any place where God leads him.

★   ★   ★

Our visiting evangelist is a Christ-anointed man. I doubt if Bro. _____ is surpassed by any man in our generation as an evangelist of power.

THE LOST GEM

I think I've lost a precious gem,
    I know not where to look;
It could be in a dresser drawer
    Or maybe in a book.

It is a rhyme that I had penned
    In camp one day at noon;
My nerves I'll need to tranquilize
    If I don't find it soon.

It could be drifting with the wind
    Or floating on a lake;
If I could only find the thing,
    It might my fortune make.

—Amy Bolding

Isn't it nice that our guest for the hour is not so careless with her literary accomplishments! For several months we have looked forward to hearing _____ speak. We are great admirers of her literary works.

Unlike the little gem in the jingle, her books and articles will live on for many years to come.

★   ★   ★

It is our great good fortune today to have with us one who is noted for his novels and stories of the great Wild West. Most of us have been thrilled by his stories of early-day history. Now we hope he will tell us all about how he writes so we may go home and start on our path to fame and fortune.

... For Men in General

The great writer Emerson said, "We only believe that which we do." The Bible says, "Faith without works is dead."

Our speaker today is a prominent Christian leader. He truly lives what he talks about. He is the president of a large and growing business but he takes time to speak often for his Lord.

★　　★　　★

Most of us fail to live up to the life and light God has given us. I want to introduce to you today a man who considers it important to know what he believes and why. He spends much time teaching others the divine truths as he sees them.

You may not agree with all he has to say but I promise you will listen to this forceful speaker and his message.

★　　★　　★

Talk is cheap because the supply always exceeds the demand, but I assure you, tonight you are not going to hear a cheap talk. Our speaker is one of the most prominent businessmen in our state. He is noted for always having something constructive to say.

★　　★　　★

We have tonight a big speaker, over six feet, in fact. But best of all he is big in many ways. He is an experienced and accomplished speaker. He not only is a clever business man but also a clever student of human nature. We are grateful that he has consented to share with us some of his knowledge and jokes. It will depend upon what kind of a person you are which you enjoy the most.

★　　★　　★

We are indeed glad to have Mr. _____ as our guest speaker tonight. I understand he is a typical young American, owes a mortgage, pays on a car, and has a wife at home busy reading the papers to see on what else they should be making payments.

Seriously, I am proud to present to you a young man who carries on the highest work in our community for the good of all.

★   ★   ★

Our speaker is the personification of unselfishness. Others, not himself, has been his primary thought, the basis of his desires and motive for his life for many years. He preaches the doctrine of a strenuous life, lived for the betterment of his community and country.

It is indeed a pleasure to introduce to you this fine member of our community.

★   ★   ★

Mr. _____ is an author of widely-known reputation. We are indeed fortunate that he could speak to us at this time. He has traveled extensively in the great Southwest and spoken to many groups. He has a loyalty to high purposes and seeks to inspire them in his audiences.

★   ★   ★

Our speaker of the hour has a pertinacity of purpose. He has many glorious achievements. His young manhood has been influenced by many intimate contacts with mature men who have been successful in their fields.

★   ★   ★

The speaker for this hour has been endowed with a love for our section of this great state. He has had access to the treasure of pioneer records in the library of the State University. He is pre-eminently qualified to speak to us on the history of our denomination in this state.

★   ★   ★

Mr. _____ is a herald who has traveled to the four corners of the earth. He is an educated and talented man. We rejoice that he could be with us today and share with us some of the excitement of his tours.

He is revered today as one of the heroes of our faith. Wherever he travels he witnesses for our Lord and Saviour.

. . . For Singers and Musicians

Music is like a window to let light into a room. We feel that music has a useful ministry in our services. We are indeed blessed today to have Mr. _____ to sing for us. He has such a beautiful voice I feel you will remember his message in song for a long time to come.

★   ★   ★

There will be music in heaven. I look forward to hearing David play his harp as other saints gather around to sing. We have today a sweet singer to lift us nearer to heaven as he sings.

★   ★   ★

The music for our evangelistic services will be under the direction of _____. He is considered one of the finest evangelistic singers in America today. He is blessed with a beautiful solo voice and as he sings you can't help feeling God speaking through him.

★   ★   ★

Mr. _____ has been called as our new Minister of Music. He served the church in _____ for a number of years. From the reports I hear they were brokenhearted when he resigned to come and work for our church.

We have been praying for God to send us the right man and now I feel we should rejoice because the Lord's will has been done.

★   ★   ★

I want to take this opportunity to present a man who always gives "good measure . . . running over." He is Mr. _____, our music director. He is a big man physically and that is well and good for he has an oversize heart. What would we do without him?

★   ★   ★

God is greatly using Mr. _____, a talented and dedicated singer. He makes the services come alive for the Lord wherever he serves. He is well trained, being a graduate of _____. His wife is also a talented musician and helps him greatly in his work.

★   ★   ★

I have known the one I am about to introduce to you for a long time and love him very much. He is a first-rate musician. His voice is as clear as a bell and you will like his arrangements very much. Come and bring your friends to hear this songbird, who sings for Christ.

★   ★   ★

I present to you today one who knows God's redemptive love. He is one who could have gone far on the stage or in the public entertainment field, yet he felt God's purpose for his life was working with Christian people to bring in the kingdom. Young and old have felt his influence and have been charmed by his lovely music.

★   ★   ★

We have with us today one who has reached maximum success in his chosen field. He realized early in life that God had given him a special talent, and as he grew and developed as a musician he determined to use his talent for God. He is a wonderful example of what God can do for a person who turns his life completely over to the Holy Spirit for guidance.

★   ★   ★

Mr. _____ is committed to serve the Lord with his many talents. Only eternity will reveal the great good he has accomplished. His commitment is motivated by his sense of dedication to the divine call.

★   ★   ★

We expect to hear the music from heaven as we start today with a new member of our church staff, our new Minister of Music. He comes to us from _____. He has a very attractive wife and _____ sweet children. I already

23

feel he has brought new life to our church just by consenting to work with us. We welcome you.

★   ★   ★

Never have I known anyone with such great Christian humility as the man I am about to welcome as our guest soloist today. I would be ungrateful indeed if I did not tell you in a small way how much his life has influenced mine.

... For Doctors

Dr. _____ has pledged himself to the development and improvement of the human body. He spends his busy days helping to alleviate pain. He also recognizes man is more than just a frail body — that man has a soul. So this very busy man takes time to speak in public meetings to help win and develop men in a spiritual way.

★　　★　　★

God not only gave Dr. _____ the gift of healing in his surgeon's hands, but he gave him a love for people. That love compels him to spend time speaking words of hope and encouragement to groups all over our city. We are indeed privileged to have him speak to us at this time.

★　　★　　★

Our speaker today is a young doctor. He is very young in the ways of the world. I asked him before the program started about mistakes. "A doctor just can't afford to make mistakes," I said.

"Oh, no? Why, once I made the mistake of curing a millionaire in three weeks."

★　　★　　★

The speaker for this hour has a great Christian testimony. He has won high acclaim in his field of medicine. He has spoken before medical conventions and is highly respected and honored by all who know him.

★　　★　　★

Would you pause for a moment to examine your heart? Dr. _____ is a heart doctor. He comes today to speak to us about matters of the heart — not the physical heart but the spiritual. He not only comes from generations of medical men, he also comes from generations of Christian men. Your spiritual heart may be troubled and need adjusting today.

★　　★　　★

Someone asked Dr. _____ why he didn't marry earlier in life. He looked fondly at his wife and smiled, "I couldn't afford it, I was in love with my best patient." He is also in love with the Lord and will thrill us with his testimony at this time.

★　　★　　★

We often pause in the busy rush of life and go to a physician for a checkup on our physical body. Dr. _____ would like to lead us today in an examination of our spiritual lives. He is a graduate of _____ Medical School and on the staff of _____ Hospital. Our town is a better place because he chose to establish a practice here.

. . . For Public Officials

One day I had occasion to talk with a popular public figure in our city. I could see he knew very little about religious affairs and thinking to help him I gave him a copy of the Gospel of John. In a few days he called me up and asked; "Say Dr. _____, you know that book you gave me written by that man John. Well, I would like to get his last name."

Our speaker today is a very prominent public official but he is also a very dedicated Christian. We are glad to welcome him at this time.

★　★　★

Mr. _____ is a well-known official in our city. The other night he was speaking to a group of parents and children on crime. His voice became hoarse and while he stopped to take a sip of water, a small boy in the audience was heard to say, "Dad, I think he needs a new needle."

★　★　★

Mr. _____ is a member of the Board of Trustees. Prior to his election he served as chairman of a number of committees. He is the son of a pioneer settler in our county. His record has been one of which he can be proud.

Before entering politics he was a successful business man.

. . . For Teachers

We thank the Lord for the response our young people have made to this fine Christian teacher. He gets paid for teaching school but seldom a day passes that he does not spend some of his time away from the schoolroom counseling with troubled youths. He would be an asset to any community so we are extremely fortunate to have him live and work in ours.

★　★　★

Mr. _____ has been teaching for many years. He tells me he has developed a philosophy about those he teaches. "If you can't change a boy or girl, accept them as they are."

People close to this teacher tell me there are very few who sit under his teaching who are not changed for the better.

★　★　★

We are indeed happy to have Mr. _____ as our speaker today. I hear he has some trouble in classes. The other day he was complaining to one of his students: "Bill, I just can't read your writing. Why don't you try to write so I can read it?"

"Well, sir, I can write better but if I wrote so you could read it you would complain about the spelling."

Well, we all know from our own youth that the life of a teacher is not all a bed of roses.

★　★　★

Dr. _____ is a professor in _____ College. He is loved and respected by all his students. His reputation as a public speaker is well known in our state.

He is a typical absent-minded professor. The other day he arrived in class with a bright red string tied around his finger.

"Dr. _____, why is that string around your finger?"

"My wife told me to tie that string on my finger so I would be reminded to mail a letter."

"Did you mail it?"

"No, she forgot to give it to me."

★   ★   ★

Miss _____ is a teacher with special training on the subject she has chosen for today. She has attended several colleges but she tells me her main training came from the practical laboratory of experience.

We will listen gladly as she tells us of her experiences and plans for the future.

★   ★   ★

Our speaker is one who promotes an extraordinary mental stimulation that is a natural result of a cheerful attitude. She is beloved by her pupils and their parents alike. We should be thankful that women of her abilities will spend their days in the classroom.

★   ★   ★

Professor _____ is a very busy man and we are glad he could come to speak to us at this time. For a while yesterday it looked as if he would have to be busier. One of his pupils named Danny came into his office with a solemn look.

"I don't want to scare you professor," Danny said, "But my dad said if I didn't get better grades, someone is due for a lickin."

★   ★   ★

Mrs. _____ has taught _____ years in _____ School. She is what I would call a second-mile teacher. She is always willing to go the second mile to help her pupils when they have difficulties. Not only is she a good teacher but she is dedicated and devoted to the cause of Christ.

★   ★   ★

Mr. _____ has accomplished much in our public schools. It has not been luck that has helped him succeed, but it has been the fact that he set some goals and refused

29

to be beaten until they were reached. He is a man of boundless courage and unlimited faith in God.

★   ★   ★

I want to introduce to you a teacher who has never stopped studying. He graduated from school a number of years ago. He still keeps up with all the latest methods of teaching and is the kind of man I would call a thinker.

. . . For Politicians

A woman politician was touring the hill country asking for votes. Late in the afternoon she came to a very poor cabin on the side of the mountain.

"I've come to ask you to support me," she started to say when a man opened the door.

He looked at her in a sad way and before she could finish he said, "I'm sorry miss; you're too late. I've been married for years."

★　★　★

Mr. ＿＿＿＿＿, speaker for the dedication of our new auditorium is so well known even those older in years would know who he was. He was born in our state near ＿＿＿＿＿. He has been educated in our state at ＿＿＿＿＿ and has served us well in public office for a number of years.

He is married and the father of ＿＿＿＿＿ children. We are indeed happy to have him speak for us at this time.

★　★　★

Young Tom Brown was hearing his first political speech. He kept noticing the speaker using the words, "renegade" and "convert." Finally he turned to a man near by and asked, "What is a renegade?"

"A man who leaves our party and goes to the other."

"Well, what is a convert?"

"A man who leaves their party and comes over to ours."

. . . For Nurses

Miss _____ first became interested in speaking to groups of people when she worked in a children's ward in the hospital.

She is a trained nurse and loves her work. Miss _____ is a member of _____ Church where she is very active.

★   ★   ★

The nurse we came to hear today is devoted to her duty. She says she could not bear to see so much suffering and sorrow if God were not her constant companion. When doctors have difficult cases they like to assign her to them because she lets them know she believes in a higher power to heal.

★   ★   ★

How wonderful it is to meet someone who spends her life helping others! Our speaker today is known for her ability to save difficult cases. One Doctor said she, "Just loves them into getting well."

Miss _____ says there is no room for self-pity in the life of a nurse. She must think first of others.

★   ★   ★

God calls many for special tasks. Miss _____ felt called to be a nurse. Firmly believing that God would provide a way for her training she enrolled in Nurse's School as soon as she finished High School. She has been successful in her determination to succeed.

... For Housewives

There are distinctive feminine traits back of our speaker's involvement in civic affairs. She is married and the mother of _____ active children.

★ ★ ★

Mrs. _____ is the wife of _____. She spends much of her spare time, if a mother and wife has any spare time, speaking on a subject dear to her heart. She is constantly amazed at the interest she finds people manifesting in her favorite subject.

★ ★ ★

Now don't be surprised by the dainty, youthful looks of our speaker. You can't tell by looks! She has a message and when she speaks people enjoy listening. She is an intelligent, modern woman who is willing to spend time making talks for the right and righteousness she feels in her heart.

★ ★ ★

When we were casting about for a speaker we hit upon the idea of asking a ordinary housewife. She is well known for accomplishing extraordinary things when she gets them on her heart. She is well known for the many drives she has led for the betterment of our community.

★ ★ ★

I am so pleased to be able to introduce to you a lovely wife and mother from our neighboring town. She will speak on a subject in which we are all interested.

. . . For Mothers-in-law

Despite all the mother-in-law jokes, I am happy to be able to introduce to you as our speaker my own dear mother-in-law. She has always been kind and patient with her in-laws. She is a teacher in _____ Church. Always she has opened her home to those in need of help or encouragement. She is the type of person who is willing to help but never interferes with the affairs of her children.

★　　★　　★

You have often heard people selecting the Mother of the Year. Well, for my choice today I want to present to you the Mother-in-law of all the years I have known her.

She is a gracious, lovely lady and I feel sure you will enjoy hearing her speak.

★　　★　　★

I want you to meet one who exemplifies the best in Christian motherhood. I would not bore you by telling all the times she has had to help me out of jams before I learned to keep house and cook.

She practices a doctrine of peace and harmony in the family and all of her children love her dearly.

May I present the mother of my husband, my mother-in-law.

★　　★　　★

There is magic in the words, I love you! Our speaker has said those words to me in times when I needed to hear them most. May I present my mother-in-law.

... For Mission Society Leaders

Mrs. _____ represents love in action. She spends much time traveling over our state organizing and speaking for the cause of missions.

Many of you have read about her work and have longed to meet so illustrious a person. Now we are privileged to have her speak to us.

★   ★   ★

Miss _____ is a marvel of ministry. She is one of the most talented people I know. All of you have read some of her articles in our mission magazine. She manages to hold a full-time job in the business world and yet spend a lot of energy promoting our mission work.

★   ★   ★

I would like to turn this meeting into an operation appreciation for our visiting speaker. The purpose of our meeting is to hear her tell us about the mission work so we will just have to say briefly, we love and appreciate you Mrs. _____ for the work you are doing.

★   ★   ★

Our denomination owes a debt of gratitude to the wonderful Christian woman who is here to speak for us at this time. At great personal sacrifice she has built our mission work to outstanding heights.

Replies to Introductions

May I express my deepest appreciation for the blessed privilege of speaking to you tonight. My faith has been re-affirmed in the future of our denomination. I have felt a new surge of joy and hope as I have watched your church in action.

★　★　★

What a wonderful introduction, I could only wish my own church people could be here to hear it. But then on the other hand they might expect more of me. You have a great pastor and I predict that as long as you "preach the word" and your main objective is everyone winning someone, your church will grow.

★　★　★

It is natural for a man to indulge in hope. So I just shall indulge in the hope that some day I shall in a small way live up to Bro. ＿＿＿＿＿'s generous introduction.

★　★　★

Thank you for your kind words of introduction. I will try not to be like the dear old minister in the South who talked for an hour on the wonderful characters in the Old Testament. Pausing for breath he said, "Now Job, where shall we put Job?"

"Job can have my seat I'm so tired I'm going home." A voice from the back spoke up and one seat was vacated.

I will take the hint if you start to leave.

★　★　★

Someone asked Mr. ＿＿＿＿＿ who was the real boss in his house.

"Well, my wife bosses the servants, and the children and the dog and cat and —"

"And you?"

"Well I can say anything I want to, to the petunias."

Now that I am away from my own church I will say anything I want to tonight. I'll bet you are ready for me to say it."

*　　*　　*

This is one of the red-letter days in my life. I have often heard of your great organization. This is my first opportunity to meet your leaders. Let me assure you I shall remember this day as long as I live. I feel fortunate to be intimately associated with your pastor since we are on several committees together.

*　　*　　*

I answer this generous introduction by making a confession. I am not really an amateur speaker. Why, I took a course in public speaking years ago. I even made a few speeches. Every time I got up to speak the people burst into gales of laughter but by the time I finished I had them all quiet; most of them slept peacefully.

*　　*　　*

A famous statesman once told his son who was planning to make a speech in school: "Be brief, be sincere, be seated."

The boy wanted to make his father proud of him so he arose to speak. "This is a brief speech, and I am sincere about the subject and I will now be seated."

I will not be quite that brief but I do have the subject for tonight on my heart.

*　　*　　*

Our beloved leader of early America once started a message by saying, "And now let us reason together, like the honest fellows we are."

If Abraham Lincoln could start speaking in this manner so can I. So, let us reason together.

*　　*　　*

This speech reminds me of a young bride. Her husband came in very cross; "The bank has returned your last check."

"Oh, goody," she giggled, "What should I buy with it next?"

This makes _____ times I have given this particular message by request.

I'm not really lazy about getting up a new one. Well at any rate I am not as lazy as a fellow I heard about back in the hills.

Pa and ma were sitting in their rocking chairs on the front porch.

"That's the funeral of old Judge Berryman going by," Ma told Pa. "Must be the longest procession we ever had in this county."

"I'd shore like to have seen it," Pa replied. "It's just too bad this chair is turned facing the other way."

★   ★   ★

I am deeply honored by your invitation to speak to your organization tonight. This church has prestige and strength. It is my prayer that you will continue under the leadership of your good pastor and be a blessing to our community.

★   ★   ★

With your indulgence I will use a few notes to keep me from rambling and taking too much of your valuable time.

★   ★   ★

Bro. _____ has said so many nice things about me I feel afraid to make much of a reply. One of us might end up like the man who lost his fingers. How did he lose his fingers?

He put them in a horse's mouth to see how many teeth he had. What happened? The horse closed his mouth to see how many fingers the man had.

So we could go on and on but let me now speak of greater matters.

★   ★   ★

Ladies and Gentlemen: I am just an ordinary person. When I get such an introduction I just have to pause and

38

wait for some of the puffed-up-pride in my heart to go down before I can speak. Thank you, for your patience.

I am proud of a country which can produce such men as the one who introduced me. He is a great fellow.

★ ★ ★

Your good pastor honors me with his good words of welcome and praise. I am happy to be in your city again.

Now I know a lot of you are sitting there wondering what I will have to say. Well I don't plan to experiment on you.

★ ★ ★

Ever since I arrived in your community this afternoon I have been impressed with your charming hospitality and kindness. It seems I have left my watch in the hotel room but Bro. _____ assures me there is a calendar on the wall in front of me. I will try not to run past tomorrow.

★ ★ ★

I appreciate the kind words of introduction. I am not an orator but like the old cow down on the farm I will give you all I've got.

★ ★ ★

Now I count it a great honor to be chosen to speak to such a large group of lovely ladies. I love women. This sure would be a dreary world without women to keep us on the right track.

★ ★ ★

Thank you for your kind words of welcome. I feel better already. I almost lost confidence in myself last week. I was the guest speaker at a banquet. About time for me to speak the Master of Ceremonies leaned over and said to me: "Would you like me to introduce you now or shall we let them enjoy themselves a little longer?"

★ ★ ★

Being in your city tonight awakens many old memories. I certainly feel honored to be asked back to my hometown

39

for an occasion like this. Most of my old teachers must have moved away.

I remember a prank we played on one of our teachers who was nearsighted. He always wore a little, black derby. One day when the wind was blowing we slipped up behind him and took off his hat. He started running down the street. Mrs. Brown hollered at him, "What do you think you are doing?"

"Chasing my hat," he puffed.

"No you're not, that is our little black hen."

He sure was surprised when he came back to school and found his hat on his desk.

★ ★ ★

Congratulations upon your accomplishments for the past year. Through your efforts you are making an important contribution to your city. I am here not to speak of the past but to urge you to accomplish still more in the future.

★ ★ ★

Last winter we had a six-inch snowfall and some of our streets became very muddy. I was walking along on the pavement when I saw a man stuck on a side street.

"Unload some and maybe it will pull out." I called to him.

"I have nothing to unload." He hollered back.

Now if I have nothing to unload in the way of a speech blame your program committee.

★ ★ ★

That was a very nice introduction. The last time I spoke in public the man who introduced me hurt my feelings. He arose and said, "This is our only speaker for the evening the rest of the program will be entertainment."

★ ★ ★

I like to speak to distinguished gentlemen. It is seldom I get a chance to say a few words, I'm married you know.

★ ★ ★

Dr. Harry Emerson Fosdick tells the story of an unmarried lady who had lived all her life in one community. One day somebody started a rumor that the lady was to be married. Her pastor stopped her on the street and asked about the coming event.

"There isn't a word of truth in it," she told him. "But thank God for the rumor."

I can't tell you that much of this fine introduction is true but, "Thank God for the rumor."

★ ★ ★

An ex-convict was walking down the street and saw his picture on the "Wanted" posters at the post office. "Well, it is good to be wanted."

Seriously, you have made me feel wanted with your kind introduction. Already in the brief moments I have been in your midst I have felt the warm fellowship of friends.

★ ★ ★

This is a wonderful age in which to live. Each day brings new excitement and drama. This opportunity to speak to you has me really excited. Your honored pastor has long been a friend of our family. It is nice to see his members and get to know you better.

★ ★ ★

Bro. _____ told me before the meeting started that he hoped my message would be like a loaf of bread: have a beginning, an end, and something in between. Well we will start with the beginning and hope we get to the end.

★ ★ ★

Now I don't think your Master of Ceremonies is a man who would exaggerate do you? Now if that be true you must believe all the kind things he said as he introduced me. I sometimes think my wife has a different opinion.

★ ★ ★

This has been a wonderful meeting. Bro. _____'s introduction was such a magnificent and flattering one now I have the difficult task of living up to it.

★　★　★

Thank you Mr. _____ for your introduction. You are a most brilliant man and exceptionally gifted with words. At times I felt I might need the dictionary to understand some of those words but believe me I felt flattered by each one.

Public Appreciation

It is a pleasure to acknowledge the kind assistance of many friends who have made my stay in your city a pleasant one.

★   ★   ★

Thanks to all of you who have rendered very important assistance by taking me places in your cars. I have enjoyed your native scenery so much because you took time to transport me.

★   ★   ★

For the considerate, helpful cooperation and encouragement of my wonderful office staff I wish to say "Thank you."

★   ★   ★

I am indeed grateful for the many courtesies shown me these past few days. A fond memory of your church will linger in my heart long after I have left here.

★   ★   ★

You are without doubt, one of the greatest groups of people with which I have ever been privileged to work. You have been an inspiration and a blessing to my life.

★   ★   ★

It is hard for me to find proper words for the tender affections that I feel in my heart for you as a congregation. Your dear pastor has been of untold inspiration to me as we have worked together these days.

★   ★   ★

These days have been a source of great and rich blessings to those of us who have been in charge of the programs. We wish to express our appreciation to all who helped make our assembly a success.

★   ★   ★

Your pastor has shown how dedicated he is by giving

himself unreservedly to the fulfilment of our purpose during this series of meetings. He is a man upon whom God has laid his hands in giving him indefatigable zeal and unswerving purpose for the bringing in of the Kingdom.

★ ★ ★

Though my friendship with Bro. _____ has not extended over a large number of years I have learned to love him dearly. I have found a real joy in my relationship with him.

★ ★ ★

My dream of spending some time with you has now been realized. I haven't enough words to express my appreciation for all the kindnesses you have showered upon me these past days.

I will long remember what a great fellow your pastor is. We have truly worked together as a team these days. He is a man who walks worthy of his high calling.

★ ★ ★

A small friend of mine was very disappointed when she learned God did not belong exclusively to the denomination with which she and her parents were affiliated.

I am disappointed that it is time for me to leave you and go to other fields. You have been most wonderful to work with and I shall look forward to being with you again soon.

★ ★ ★

What a grand and glorious person Mr. _____ is. I would indeed be an ungrateful person if I did not take a moment to say a few words about the way he has worked to make our project a success. I know God will bless and reward him for his unselfish devotion to the cause.

★ ★ ★

Let me say a few words of appreciation for a man whose persistency and enthusiasm has made our campaign a successful one. He accepted his work as a challenge and his faith in the right of the cause has carried us over many obstacles to success.

★   ★   ★

How we do thank Mr. _____ for helping us cut loose our moorings and reach for a goal. His zeal and leadership will direct us to the fulfilment of our dream.

Under his leadership we are headed for bigger and better accomplishments.

★   ★   ★

We wish to express our appreciation to Dr. _____ for taking time to speak to us today. He has the practical knowledge and ability to present his theories in a manner which is interesting and easy to understand.

★   ★   ★

It has certainly been a blessing to have Dr. _____ as our guest today. He is nationally known as an authority on the subject about which he has spoken.

★   ★   ★

Mr. _____ has contacts with many successful men. He has personal interviews and thereby learns some of the secrets of their success. We are indeed grateful that he has given us some of his findings condensed in his lecture tonight.

★   ★   ★

We wish to thank Mrs. _____ for her generous gift to our organization. She is a fine Christian woman and never does she forget that she has a story to tell. When she cannot go herself she helps to send others.

★   ★   ★

We express our gratitude to one who holds aloft the torch of Christian culture. He is an outstanding citizen of the Kingdom. He has spoken to us in truth and in love. He is profoundly spiritual and his influence will inspire us as we make plans for the future.

Thanks to Special Committees

For those who have labored as a committee in the past days I wish to express the appreciation of our entire congregation. The following people were members of the committee: ——————, ——————.

★　★　★

The members of the —————— Committee have been very faithful. In all times and places they have conducted themselves with dignity and have been true and brave in making plans for our church.

★　★　★

Our committee on —————— may now rest from their labors. They have worked long and well. Their works will follow them. We wish to thank them for planning so well and accomplishing the task we set before them.

★　★　★

I cannot say enough to really show our appreciation to the committee on ——————. They truly worked together as co-workers with God. At all meetings they were in prayer before they made any decisions. Among the whole group, and it necessarily had to be a large committee, not one was ever known to show lazy complacency or selfish purpose.

★　★　★

With great care and study this committee has applied themselves to their task. We thank each of you for your time and service.

★　★　★

We certainly owe deep gratitude to the Advertising Committee for the splendid job they have accomplished promoting our special day services.

It is a thrill to see such a large crowd here and much of

the credit for this attendance goes to our Advertising Committee.

★   ★   ★

Inside me there is a warm glow when I see such Christian enthusiasm manifested as we have here today. I wish to thank the Arrangements Committee for the splendid way they have promoted the plans for this happy day. Without their careful planning we would never have been so well organized.

★   ★   ★

This banquet tonight realizes one of my life's ambitions. The attendance is splendid and the program has been superb. We wish to recognize the following committees: The Food Committee, the Decorations Committee, the Program Committee, and last but in no wise least, the Clean-up Committee. Will all the members of these committees stand?

★   ★   ★

Please convey my thanks to the Hospitality Committee. They made my visit in your city very pleasant and I wish to express my deepest appreciation to each of them.

Welcomes

... To a Group

We are happy indeed to have with us today a group of young people who belong to the _____ club. We are grateful to God for laying upon the hearts of men and women the need for such organizations. We thank the leaders for bringing this group to worship with us today.

We would like all of you to stand so that we may know you better. Thank you, we will remember your organization in our prayers.

★ ★ ★

We are happy to report that in our services today we have Professor _____ and a group of students from _____ College. The teachers and pupils at this school are doing a tremendous job. We are proud to be able to say this school belongs to our denomination.

★ ★ ★

We are continuously amazed at the wonderful blessings of the Lord upon the work of our church. Visiting with us today is a group from one of our mission churches. We have eagerly watched this child of our church grow.

Later in the service they will have opportunity to tell us more about the work of the mission.

★ ★ ★

We are honored to have a troop of Boy Scouts here to worship with us. These fine boys will be the men of tomorrow. They will serve their community better because they have been trained in the art of scouting.

... To a New Pastor and Family

We have looked forward to the coming of our new pastor with great anticipation and joy. Bro. _____ we feel you are God's leader for us at this time, sent to us after much prayer and searching.

Rest assured that we will seek to follow your leadership in the affairs of our church. The life of our church will be richer and fuller because we have you and your good family to live and work among us.

Feel free to call upon us for any help you need getting settled in our community. We may not always please you and you may step on our toes in some of your messages but with the help of our Heavenly Father we expect to work together in love for the growth of the Kingdom of God.

★　　★　　★

Dear new pastor and family, today we become the flock for which you are responsible. We are your congregation to direct and lead. Your task is both great and will at times be difficult. We welcome you with all our hearts and hope you will learn to love us in spite of our shortcomings. We need you very much and have prayed diligently for God to send us a leader.

... To a New Educational Director

We are so glad to have you as our new Educational Director. We trust to you the planning and promoting of our Sunday School and Training Program. We have the utmost confidence you will lead us in a great and wonderful way.

You come to us with good training and an accumulation of experience. We will expect you to make many decisions for our organizations and we will try to back you in those decisions.

We feel that God has led us to call you as our leader in this field and know you will need courage and a deep love of God to put up with some of our faults.

You have not accepted an easy place but we are so grateful for your coming. We will not promise always to do all you ask but we will promise to love and pray for you.

★ ★ ★

We are grateful to our Heavenly Father for laying it upon your heart to come and work with us. We know you loved the people with whom you have been working but our need is great. We love you for coming and will try to make our work together pleasant and happy. We know you will do a tremendous job with the help of our prayer and backing.

... To a Visiting Pastor's Wife

Mrs. _____ is a faithful, dedicated pastor's wife. She is loved and honored by all who know her. She has taught classes in the churches where her husband has been pastor. She has an outstanding Christian spirit and attitude. Her influence lingers with all who know her. We are grateful for her presence here today.

... To Old Friends

A few years ago a dedicated family moved away from our city. Precious memories lingered with us after they departed. Today the _____ family are back visiting in our services. You are always welcome. We remember your days here with joy and hope you will always come back when opportunity affords itself.

★   ★   ★

In the language of the poet Tennyson, of England, we wish to express a few thoughts.

> More things are wrought by prayer
> Than this world dreams of. Wherefore let thy voice
> Rise like a fountain for me night and day
> For what are men better than sheep or goats,
> That nourish a blind life within the brain,
> If knowing God, they lift not hands of prayer,
> Both for themselves and those who call them friend.
> For so the whole round world is every way
> Bound by gold chains about the feet of God.

Installation Services

... For General Officers

(Have all officers and chairmen seated in front of the audience. At one side of the stage place a small table covered with a white cloth.)

Presiding officer, or installing officer:

Just a clean white cloth on a bare table before you. You might be thinking, "What does a table with a white cloth signify to our organization? Let us view it as a white field ready indeed unto a rich harvest. Each new officer for the coming year must see his task as something vital and necessary if this table is to be adorned with the vessels necessary for its beauty and usefulness.

Now we will adorn this table with instruments to be used in our organization this coming year.

Will the president, Mrs. _____, come and stand by the table?

Mrs. _____, our new president. We will place on this table a vase of flowers. These flowers represent the beauty and gracious presiding you will carry out this coming year. You always will be the centerpiece of the organization, but you will use the other officers to make the organization function properly.

Mrs. _____, the new vice-president. We place on the table a plate to represent the fact that you are in charge of enlistment for this organization. Fill this plate with new members. You can do this by going out into the highways and hedges and compelling them to come in. Will you pledge your loyalty to this task by standing beside the president?

Secretary, Mrs. —————. On the table for you we place a saucer.

Treasurer, Mrs. —————. We place in the saucer a cup. Will you two ladies stand by the president and vice-president?

The cup and saucer just naturally go together, so does the work of the secretary and treasurer. In keeping the records, minutes, roll call, and financial reports, we hope this cup will run over with good deeds, tithes, and offerings.

Social leader, Mrs. —————. We place an empty glass on the table for you. The glass stands more or less alone and above the other instruments. The social leader must fill this glass with a happy spirit among the women. You will not only have charge of the social activities but you must try to promote good fellowship at each meeting.

Group Leaders. Will the group leaders come and stand by the other officers? For you useful and busy workers we place on the table a fork and a napkin. They are used most often of all instruments. There will be a task for you at each meeting. You will see that your group has been notified of all meetings.

Reporter, Mrs. —————. Will you too stand by the other officers? For you we place on the table a spoon. The spoon of publicity. You will spoon out the news to the local newspaper.

Pianist, or chorister, Mrs. —————. For you we place a knife on the table. Your music will be sharp and clear.

What a lovely table! But what kind of a table would we have without a hostess. Will the teacher, Mrs. ————— take her place at the table? She prepares the food each week. She it is who feeds us from the bread of life.

> I have a hidden table
> That I must tend with care
> And fill with lovely growing
>   things,
> Least weeds should gather there.

> May sweetness, kindness, mercy and
>   joy be in each part,
> To grace this hidden table,
> The table of my heart.

Prayer of Dedication:

Bless each new officer today. May they determine to fill the place assigned them with the very best of their skill and ability.

Take away the indifference in the hearts of some members and inspire them to work hard to make our organization the greatest ever this year.

. . . For Men's Organizations

(Presiding or installing officer will have a large flannel board on the stage before the meeting starts. If a flannel board is not available, a piece of peg board with hooks can be used.

Ask the officers to be installed to sit in a circle facing the audience.

Leader, place a large white or red cross on the flannel board in the center. Talk about Christ on the cross, then quote a verse of the song, Must Jesus Bear the Cross Alone.)

> Must Jesus bear the cross alone,
>   And all the world go free?
> No, there's a cross for every one,
>   And there's a cross for me.
>
> The consecrated cross I'll bear
>   Till death shall set me free,
> And then go home my crown to wear,
>   For there's a crown for me.
>   —Thomas Shepherd

Many great leaders have been successful because they knew how to distribute the load of responsibility to others. The wise leader often lets others represent him, prepare information and programs for him and help him in many ways.

Jesus did not plan to save the world without help. He multiplied his hands by selecting twelve helpers at first, then later seventy, then as the years have rolled by helpers have selected other helpers until today there are countless thousands of helpers for the cause of Christ.

As the new officers in this organization you will multiply the hands of Christ by filling the place assigned to you to the very best of your ability.

(As the installing officer calls the name of each officer he will place a hand on the flannel board pointing toward the cross.)

For the president:

We think of our president as our leader, so, for him we will place a large hand at the foot of the cross.

How fine it is to start something new if it is good. We will follow the new leadership of our president. We will expect to have a joyful and fruitful year under his leadership.

For the vice-president:

There is a story told of a man who wished very much to clear his field of rocks. Having no modern equipment he was rolling the rocks on a sled and letting his faithful horse pull the load. Finally all the rocks but one were out of the field. The man tried and tried but he could not lift the rock onto the sled. Finally he told the men and boys in the neighborhood he would give a prize to the one who could load the rock for him. Many friends gathered and each in turn tried to move the rock. Finally after all had failed a small man stepped forward and said, "I can move the rock if you will all follow my instructions."

"Now each man take the prize pole he has been using and we will all prize at one time," he instructed.

All working together soon had the huge stone rolled on the sled.

If this president is to be successful he must have many hands working together. So we will place a smaller hand on the board for the Vice-president.

(Call each officer and as each is mentioned place a hand on the board for him. Before they are all seated again read the following verse.)

"Whatsoever thy hand findeth to do, do it with thy might" (Ecclesiastes 9:10).

57

(Before having the dedicatory prayer read the poem, The Touch of the Master's Hand. A copy may be found in the book, Day by Day with Amy Bolding, *p. 154.)*

Now I will place some hands for you who are not officers. You too will fill an important place by holding up the hands of those who have been installed in the offices of this organization.

(Have all rise and hold hands as they sing a verse of the song, "Blest Be the Tie That Binds.")

Closing prayer of dedication led by outgoing president or pastor.

(Suitable hands may be made by tracing a child's hand on tan construction paper. Make light pink nails. Paste a small strip of sandpaper on the back of each so they will cling to the flannel.)

Dedications

... Of a Christian Home

Conscious that, "Except the Lord build the house, they labor in vain that build it."
(Response) We dedicate this house.

With the prayer that it may be safe from all manner of calamity such as fire and storm.
(Response) We dedicate this house to serve our Lord.

Thou shalt teach these words diligently.
(Response) We dedicate this house to religious instruction.

Teach me thy ways, O Lord.
(Response) We dedicate this house to religious discipline.

Let the words of my mouth and the meditations of my heart be acceptable in thy sight.
(Response) We dedicate this house to religious conversation.

And these words shall be in thy heart and thou shalt talk of them.
(Response) We dedicate this house to religious hospitality.

When thou sittest in thine house.
(Response) We dedicate this house to religious worship.

When thou walkest by the way and when thou liest down and when thou risest up.
(Response) We dedicate all our activities in this house to be honorable unto thy name.

Prayer of Dedication:
   Come into this house, O Lord, upon this happy day, and

remain with us through the rest of our lives. Help us to realize how good and gracious you were to make this new home possible. May we ever be happy to share the blessings of this house. Help us to appreciate our privileges. May all who come this way receive a blessing. Place a cloak of happiness around our home today and dwell with us.

HOME

Life's entirely without purpose
    For him who would live alone —
Whatever be the dwelling place,
    It cannot thus be a home.

Home means living for another —
    Working for their greatest good —
Thus building God-like character,
    Where once selfishness has stood.

For home is more than living space —
    Home is more than wood and stone —
There must be much love and giving,
    And you can't have these alone.
                    —Edward V. Wood
                        Dallas, Texas

... Of a Building

Pastor: This is the day the Lord hath made. Let us rejoice and be glad in it.

People: The Lord hath done great things for us, whereof we are glad.

Pastor: For the faith and vision and sacrifice of thy people who have through the years desired to build this house.

People: We thank thee, Gracious Father.

Pastor: Being graciously proposed by the hand of God to finish the work which in his providence we were called upon to perform.

People: We dedicate this building and consecrate our lives.

Pastor: To the glory of God, the Father, to the honor of our Lord and Saviour Jesus Christ, and to the praise of the Holy Spirit, source of life and light.

People: We dedicate this building and consecrate our lives.

Pastor: For the preaching of the gospel of the Lord Jesus Christ, at home and around the world.

People: We dedicate this building and consecrate our lives.

Pastor: For the practice of prayer, remembering the Lord's house shall be called the House of Prayer.

People: We dedicate this house and consecrate our lives.

Pastor: For the purpose of winning men, women, and youth to a saving knowledge of the Lord Jesus Christ.

People: We dedicate this house and consecrate our lives.

Pastor: For the nurture of youth and the enrichment of the home.

People: We dedicate this house and consecrate our lives.

Pastor: For the comfort of the bereaved and the uplift of the heavy laden,

People: We dedicate this house and consecrate our lives.

Pastor: For the observance of ordinances in rememberance of our Lord, who gave them to his church,

People: We dedicate this house and consecrate our lives.

Pastor: For the enrichment of our lives, both as Christians and citizens, and the uplift of humanity, church and state.

People: We dedicate this building and consecrate our lives.

Pastor and people:

We now, the people of this church and congregation, compassed about with so great a cloud of witnesses, grateful for our heritage, mindful of the sacrifices of our fathers, conscious of our obligations to the present and of our responsibility to posterity, do covenant in the presence of God and one another, to walk humbly together in service and love, so help us God.

I want it to be a church that is
   a lamp to the path of pilgrims,
leading them to goodness, truth
   and beauty. It will be, if I am.

It is composed of people like me.
   We make it what it is.
It will be friendly, if I am.
   It's pews will be filled, if
I help fill them.

It will do a great work, if I work.

It will make generous gifts to many causes,
    If I am a generous giver.
It will bring other people into it's
    Worship and fellowship,
If I bring others.

It will be a church of loyalty
    And love, of fearlessness and faith,
And a church with a noble spirit —
    If I who make it what it is,
Am filled with these.

Therefore, with the help of God,
    I shall dedicate myself to the
Task of being all of the things that
    I want my church to be.

. . . Of a Library

Libraries date back to early history. The public library was a Roman institution, but was destroyed by fires set by barbarians.

Christian people are interested in books and many churches have libraries. Our own church has planned for a number of years to establish a library for use of our members. Today we see the fulfillment of that dream.

Reading good books can make many hours pleasant as well as fruitful. We are thankful to be able to provide such a well-equipped library for our people.

As we know them today, public libraries are not much over one hundred years old. Church libraries are much newer than that. So you see, we are proud to be advancing with the times, almost ahead of the times.

Today we dedicate this library to the edification and joy of all who enter here.

★   ★   ★

When we first began talking about establishing a church library people felt skeptical. To establish a library is a large undertaking, yet we felt it was an assignment from the Lord. An assignment to provide good literature for our members to read. As we come for this dedication service I feel God has richly blessed our efforts. We are happy today to dedicate this library to God for His glory, to the people for their use and pleasure.

... Of a Musical Instrument

At last the musical instrument _____ for which we saved and worked has arrived. We are so happy. The fine quality of the instrument we dedicate today, will catch the attention of the music-loving public in our city.

The generous gifts of those who made this instrument possible will long be remembered. Not only will this instrument make beautiful music but it is beautiful to look at. It harmonizes with the other furnishings of our building. It is truly a nice addition to the physical equipment of our church.

. . . Of a Pastor's Study and Church Office

For too many years our pastor and office staff have had inadequate office space and equipment. We have heard very little complaining from them, therefore it makes us doubly glad today to come for the dedication of a new office and pastor's study.

We pause but momentarily today to dedicate this new facility of our church. We feel our dear pastor will spend many hours here praying and preparing for the ongoing of his work.

It will give us joy to know he is here in this pleasant study; to know we may call at almost any time and secure his help or services. How happy we are to pause for prayer in this pleasant place.

... Greetings to People on Day of Dedication

Today is a great day in the life of our church. We have many visitors as well as members present to share the blessings of this occasion with us. It is a real joy to have our friends visit us for this opening day of our new building.

Many have made real sacrifices in helping financially to make this building possible. We ask God's blessings upon all who have given so unselfishly.

With a continuation of the same spirit there will be glorious days before us in the growth of our church.

★　★　★

The day of dedication for our new building is the culmination of many months, yes even years, of careful planning. We had many faithful committees working on plans and fund raising. Not a group fell down on their duties. Truly today I can thank all of you for working together without discord to make this building possible.

This beautiful structure will stand as a memorial to the membership of _____ Church. This building truly manifests the devotion and love for the cause of Christ.

At this time I would like us to read in unison I Corinthians 15:58.

. . . Appreciation on a Day of Dedication

The pastor and the church as a body wish to express appreciation to each member of the church and it's organizations for the wonderful spirit which has prevailed throughout the financing and construction of this new Educational Building.

Your generosity of means, time, and effort has been inspiring, and in many cases, sacrificial.

Willingness and vision in planning, unity of purpose, cooperative endeavor, and the sustained drive to completion, have been thrilling to witness.

"I thank my God upon every remembrance of you, Always in every prayer of mine for you all making request with joy, For your fellowship in the gospel from the first day until now." — Phillipians 1:3-5

★   ★   ★

The membership of our church rejoices in the presence of all former members, and friends of the church. Our happiness is increased today by your being here to rejoice with us. From the depths of our hearts comes a welcome to you this happy day of our church dedication.

★   ★   ★

With deep gratitude we wish to acknowledge the flowers, telegrams, and letters sent from friends to congratulate our church upon reaching the time for the dedication of our building.

A Marriage Ceremony

Scripture:

"Wives, submit yourselves unto your own husbands, as unto the Lord." — Colossians 3:19

"For the husband is the head of the wife, even as Christ is the head of the church; and he is the saviour of the body."
— Ephesians 5:23

"Husbands love your wives, even as Christ also loved the church and gave himself for it." — Ephesians 5:25

"For this cause shall a man leave his father and mother, and shall cleave unto his wife, and they twain shall be one flesh?" — Matthew 19:5

"Wherefore they are no more twain, but one flesh. What therefore God hath joined together, let not man put asunder."
— Matthew 19:6

★   ★   ★

Dearly beloved: We have assembled here this beautiful evening *(or morning)* in the presence of God with our friends to witness the exchange of the marriage vows between this stalwart and dedicated young man and this talented and precious young woman.

God's Holy Word teaches us that marriage is of divine appointment and approval. In the beginning, God, in His wisdom and love, saw in the Garden of Eden, that it was not good for man to be alone, so he gave him a woman to be his companion and helper for life.

Jesus at Cana honored a marriage festival with his presence and wrought there the beginning of his miracles.

Marriage is a joyous occasion, connected in our hearts with the magic charm of home and with all that is most

69

pleasant and attractive in the most tender and sacred relationship known to this life.

So it is ordained of God that a man should leave his father and his mother and cleave only and always unto his wife, they twain being one.

Who brings _____ to be married to _____?

(Father of bride answers and then takes his seat.)

We trust that it is love that has brought you together and it is love that must sustain you. God's Word in a modern version describes it:

> "Love is so patient and so kind;
> Love never boils with jealousy;
> It never boasts, is never puffed with pride;
> It does not act with rudeness,
> or insist upon its rights;
> It never gets provoked, it never
> harbors evil thoughts;
> Is never glad when wrong is done,
> But always glad when truth prevails;
> It bears up under anything,
> It exercises faith in everything,
> It gives us power to endure in
> everything.
>
> Love never fails: . . .
> And so these three: faith, hope, and
> love endure,
> But the greatest of them is love."
>
> (Williams, I Cor. 13:4-8, 13)

Since marriage is an appointment of God, it is to be entered into thoughtfully and prayerfully, and the vows are to be broken only by death.

In token of your having chosen each other out of all the world beside, you will please join your right hands for the vows.

Do you _____, take _____, to be your wedded wife, to have and to hold from this day forward, for better or for worse, for richer or for poorer, in sickness and in health, and do you promise, in the presence of God and these witnesses, to love, to cherish, to honor, to protect, and to pray for her, through all the changing scenes of life, and forsaking all others, to be faithful unto her so long as you both shall live?

Answer _____.

Do you _____, take _____ to be your wedded husband, to have and to hold from this day forward, for better or for worse, for richer or for poorer, in sickness and in health, and do you promise in the presence of God and these witnesses, to love, to cherish, to honor, and to pray for him, through all the changing scenes of life, and, forsaking all others, to be faithful unto him so long as you both shall live?

Answer _____.

_____. What token of your love do you bring?

(Best man hands ring to groom who hands it to the minister.)

The wedding band is the outward and visible symbol of an inward and a spiritual union, forever binding loving and loyal hearts in Holy Wedlock.

As an emblem, may it be significant in your wedded relationship.

Do you _____, give this ring as a token of your love for _____?

Will you _____, receive this ring and promise to wear it as a symbol of your love for _____?

Repeat after me:

With this ring I thee wed, and pledge my heart's true love to thee, according to the teachings of God's Holy Word. Amen.

_____. What token of your love do you bring?

71

(Maid of honor hands ring to bride, bride hands it to minister.)

As this circle is of materials least tarnished, most enduring, pure and precious, may it symbolize in its pledge your mutual affection one for the other.

(Repeat the same vows for girl as given above for man.)

Since you _____, and you _____, have covenanted to unite your lives in holy wedlock, declaring the same before God and these witnesses, now therefore, by the authority vested in me as a minister of the gospel, in the holy hush of this sacred moment, I pronounce you husband and wife, in the name of the Father, and of the Son, and of the Holy Spirit, reminding you of the words of our blessed Saviour: "What therefore God hath joined together, let not man put asunder."

Go forth to share the joys and sorrows of life and to pray about them together. May you dedicate your home even now to Christ and dedicate yourselves to faithfully serve Him. May you deliberately plan each to bless the life of the other and to bless the world.

May the recurring years bring each of you the joys of "Home Sweet Home," ever love's paradise.

In the words of the ancient benediction:

"The Lord bless thee and keep thee.
The Lord make His face to shine
upon thee and be gracious unto thee.
The Lord lift up His countenance upon thee
and give thee peace." — Numbers 6:24

Let us pray.

Dear Lord, crown this new home with divine favor. Give to them temporal and spiritual blessings. Make their home a veritable oasis of peace and inspiration for those who pass their way. May the sun always shine brightly on their pathway, and all the hours of their lives be hallowed with a heavenly radiance. We pray in the name of Jesus Christ our Lord. Amen.

Special Prayers

Oh, for a passionate passion for souls!
Oh, for a pity that yearns!
Oh, for a love that loves unto death!
Oh, for a fire that burns!
Oh, for prevailing power in prayer
That pours itself out for the lost;
Victorious prayer in the Saviour's name!
Oh, for a Pentecost!

—Anonymous

★   ★   ★

Our Father, if we have been negligent Christians, forgive us, and help us to show our gratitude for the innumerable blessings you have showered upon us. May we show our gratitude by living lives wholly yielded to thee. Amen.

★   ★   ★

The Lord is nigh unto all them that call upon him. — Psalm 145:18

. . . At a Time of Doubt or Sorrow

Lord, may we today take hope as our daily companion. Fill our hearts with faith in thee. Let joy be our portion and take away all our worries. We are firm in the knowledge that thou wilt not fail us, that thy love will last and thou wilt be with us until every ill is past. Amen.

. . . New Year

As a new year is beginning we would steal away from our daily cares to speak to thee our Lord. We wish to acknowledge our past weaknesses and mistakes, our failures and frustrations, our moments of despair and greed. We have at times been little and selfish. There have been days when we had little faith.

Forgive us our sins and cleanse us from all unrighteousness. With the help of the Holy Spirit may we chart a new course for a more effective life in the coming year. Amen.

. . . Commitment Day

May we resolve that we will not live in vain. The dictates of our Christian hearts speak loudly to us and we wish to be obedient to thy call. We have no promise of tomorrow but as we close our eyes at night may we resolve that each new day granted us will be pledged for the glory of God. Amen.

★   ★   ★

Prayer is so simple.
It is like quietly opening a door —
And slipping into the very Presence of God.
There — in the stillness —
To listen for His voice;
    Perhaps to petition,
Or only — to listen;
    It matters not;
Just to be there,
    In His presence,
      Is prayer.

. . . Christmas

Father, we thank thee for the Christmas season. It is a season of gladness for most of us. Give our hearts concern for those in need at this season. May we plan to give as well as receive gifts. To all the packages we see in our homes may we add a gift of ourselves. As we think of the gift Jesus made for us may we be filled with concern for others.

Let there be in our hearts, as we again regard the Christ of the cradle, new faith and hope for a better world. Touch and make beautiful our lives at this season. Amen.

★   ★   ★

We offer a prayer at this Christmas time that God will bless each home represented here. Give to each a lasting happiness founded upon love for Christ. Let the peace and happiness of Christmas be theirs today and each day throughout the coming year. May the meaning of Christmas be stronger and brighter than ever before.

Help us keep our observance of the holidays in such a way that will be well-pleasing to thee. Bless our loved ones who are far away and those close at hand. Fill us with happy contentment and peace. Amen.

★   ★   ★

At this season give us grace to share our joys with others, give us sympathetic hearts for those in need of material help, give us comforting words for those in need of comfort at this happy season. Amen.

. . . Easter

We thank thee, Father, for the hope of immortality that comes anew at Easter time. May the vision of a risen Saviour be bright in our hearts today. Help us to tell others of the living Lord. Clothe us anew with the realization of an endless life.

The mystery of the resurrection is deep and we do not understand all things, but dear God, make real the hope of eternal life in our hearts at this season. Amen.

. . . Thanksgiving

Our Father, who hast opened the windows of heaven and given us blessings far beyond our capacity to receive, we come to thank thee today.

Bless our homes and our families. Give us compassion for those who are not so blessed as we.

Bless today our great nation and may we ever strive to keep it great. Forgive the wrongs we often impose on others and help us to live in peace and love for our fellow men.

Bless our schools and our churches. May we ever strive to make them as thou would have them be. We thank thee for freedom and give us determination to ever stand for the Christian way of life.

Miscellaneous

... Tribute to a Pastor's Wife

We have in our services today one of the greatest women I have ever met in my many years of gospel ministry. With the exception of my own dear companion, I have long regarded her as the most ideal pastor's wife in my acquaintance.

When one spends some time with this dear lady he goes away feeling he has been in the company of an angel. Her husband is a great man and has spread much influence for good. He carries the name of a great man in our denomination but back of him carrying the load of home and family has been this good woman.

So long as there are women like Mrs. _____ in the parsonage the world will be worth preserving for they will make it so.

★　★　★

Someone has aptly said, "To have friends you must be friendly."

We have one in our congregation who is always friendly. She greets us each Sunday with a happy smile and all freely tell her their problems and ask her help and advice. It is a joy for us today to pay tribute to one we love so much as our pastor's wife.

... Thanks for Special Favors

> Hidden and deep and never dry,
>   Or flowing or at rest,
> A living spring of love doth lie
>   In every human breast.
> All else may fail that soothes the
>   heart,
>   All save that fount alone;
> With that and life we never part;
>   For life and love are one.
>   —Arnold

★   ★   ★

Thank you for your kindness in being our chauffeur and host and for all the other kind things you did to make our stay in _____ enjoyable. It was a real inspiration to have fellowship with your growing dynamic church.

We pray God's continued blessings upon you and hope you'll come to see us some of these days.

★   ★   ★

I am writing on behalf of _____ student body. We want to thank you so very much for coming to speak to us. I am sure we all received a blessing from it. We hope you will speak to us again very soon.

★   ★   ★

Thank you so much for inviting us into your lovely home. We felt honored indeed.

You are such thoughtful and wonderful people, it is a pleasure to visit with you.

... Greetings for Special Days

We, the Church Staff, take this means of telling you how earnest is our wish for each of you that this be the most joyous and Christian Christmas that you, your family and friends have ever known.

We pledge to you at this Christmas Season, and the New Year ahead, that we shall work and serve our Saviour and his church to the best of our abilities. Would you join us that each of our members will make the same vow.

(Copied from the First Baptist Church bulletin, Lubbock, Texas.)

★ ★ ★

To the faculty and administrators of _____ School, the Senior Class of _____ wishes to say "Thanks." For all the friendliness, smiles, courtesies, and companionship you have given us. If it were not for such wonderful instructors as you, we could not have had the many happy memories in our school life recollection.

As we leave _____, we leave as one entering into the portals of a new life, truly a commencement on many new and different experiences, but we carry with us a portion of the high ideals you, the faculty and administrators, have instilled within us.

. . . Written Thank You Notes

Dear Friend:

Thank you for the lovely card and your visit. Your gentleness and kindness makes your life one I would like to emulate. Will you please pray that I may be a better Christian when I am well again.

★　　★　　★

Dear Mrs. _____:

We would like to thank you for the wonderful book you sent as a gift. We try to read some from it each day.

★　　★　　★

Dear _____:

Your friendship has been like a golden key. The key of your friendship has opened wide the door to such special happiness; happiness unknown to me before. I will have other friends but always I will love and appreciate the friendship of the one who told me about Jesus my Lord.

★　　★　　★

Dear Pastor:

During the last year we have left many things undone but as a new year starts we want to be more thoughtful and express our love and appreciation for the wonderful work you are doing in our church and community.

★　　★　　★

Dear _____:

Your gift is a treasure I shall always enjoy. You were so thoughtful to send it. May God bless you.

★　　★　　★

Dear _____:

From a heart filled with sincere appreciation we thank you for the beautiful service you conducted for our loved one.

80

You brought us much comfort and we shall be everlastingly grateful.

★   ★   ★

Dear Friends:

The thought came to me that I need not wait until you are ready to leave our church to let you know how much we appreciate you and always will.

You have meant so much to our family. Your kind words, and happy, understanding smile have brought cheer to the hearts of many.

Thank you sincerely for what your life has meant to us.

★   ★   ★

Dear _____:

My family and I want you to know how much we appreciated your interest in us while I was in the hospital. Thank you for every visit and prayer. We have learned to love you very much because you are so kind and thoughtful.

... Reply to an Introduction by a Former Pastor

Good pastor and members of your congregation, it was so thoughtful of your pastor to ask me back today to share in the dedication of your new building.

The music we have already enjoyed has made my trip worthwhile. The handclasp of old friends as I came into the building has warmed my heart.

★   ★   ★

Dear people, I am so glad to be back in your midst again. Several have told me already what a fine pastor you have now and I rejoice with you in your growth.

Your pastor has been useful in many capacities and I have enjoyed the fellowship with him. He was indeed kind to invite me for this special day.

★   ★   ★

It is a joy today to be welcomed once again into your church. I have a very tender place in my heart for you good people. It is a blessing to see how you are working and growing as a congregation.

★   ★   ★

In the ranks of our denomination your pastor is known and respected. Already I can see what a great pastor he has been for you. He was indeed thoughtful to invite me here today.

... When a Pastor Has to Say Goodbye

It is with mixed emotions that we present to you a few parting words. We feel God has called us to other fields and it is best to go. We are unable adequately to express our sincere appreciation for the privilege of serving as your pastor these past _____ years.

You have been most encouraging, cooperative and kind. We shall always be grateful.

We thank you for every prayer you have offered and for every good and encouraging word you have spoken during these past years. You have honored the Saviour and added to the spirit and progress of our church. We are grateful for the various ways by which you have been a blessing to the members of our family.

We shall rejoice with you in the future as you go on to attain greater heights and nobler victories. May your church ever grow stronger and serve the Lord in greater ways.

★ ★ ★

Today is my last service with you dear people. I shall always be grateful for the years we have had together. You have been patient with my mistakes and generous in your praise when I succeeded. May God continue to pour his richest blessings upon your church. I covet your prayers as I enter a new field of service.

... A Parting Word from the Pastor's Wife

You have made our hearts happy many times. Today we are sad at the thought of leaving our dear friends. I wish to express to each of you our gratitude and deep appreciation for the many kind things you have done for us during the years past.

Serving you has been a joy and blessing. Thank you for the many times you have prayed for us as we tried to serve your church.

Now we must turn our faces toward a new field and start all over to make new friends. We have come to the close of our fellowship together but will you remember us in your prayers as we certainly shall continue to ask God's blessings on this dear congregation.

★ ★ ★

If ever anyone deserved the finest and best I feel it is this dear church. Our years with you have been filled with happiness and joy. We have had troubles but you have been ever faithful to stand by. You have had troubles and we have tried to be a strength and comfort to you.

Though we will be miles away from you in a few days we will always feel that you are that special church and people who have helped mold and shape our lives as Christian workers.

Today I wish for you all the success and happiness you deserve. Will you always keep our memory in a little corner of your hearts?

... Greetings from the Pastor at Christmas

Since Christmas is a time of giving, our minds turn in that direction. The greatest gift I have ever received is salvation through Christ. There are other gifts also for which I am inexpressibly grateful. Among them are your love, your friendship, your prayers in my behalf, and the numerous words of encouragement which you have written or spoken to me.

And now I wish you, my dearly beloved people, along with your loved ones, a happy, joyful Christmas season.

May Christ be in your midst and heaven in your hearts.

★ ★ ★

As an expression of our deep appreciation for the very pleasant association we enjoy with you, we send the warmest greetings at this Christmas time.

We value your friendship highly and have only good will in our hearts for you and yours at this season.

★ ★ ★

May the glory of the risen Christ abide in your hearts this blessed Christmas season. You have added to our daily lives this past year lots of loving and giving. We hope your Christmas will be filled with happiness and cheer. Accept our best wishes for a blessed Christmas and New Year.

... Presenting a Gift

Please accept this small gift as a token of our love and appreciation for all you have done to further the progress of our organization.

★ ★ ★

Some years ago a family came to our city and started working in our church. They have lived exemplary lives before us. They have never made us sad until the day they told us they would be leaving. As a token of our love and esteem we wish to present to them this gift of money. We felt there would be many needs as you move and start life in a new place. Along with the offering goes lots and lots of love for each of you.

★ ★ ★

I take pleasure in presenting to you on behalf of your associates in this office a token of our love and respect for you.

★ ★ ★

Miss _____, you have been a competent and well-trained worker in our organization. It is with regret we see you leaving us. In order that you often may be reminded of your days spent here we wish to present you with this gift.

★ ★ ★

I consider it an honor to be the one chosen to present this token of our esteem to you.

... Acceptance and Thanks

You make me think of the maiden lady who had been courted by an old bachelor for a number of years. Finally he asked her to marry him.

"Oh, Henry, this is so sudden!" she exclaimed.

This wonderful gift is such a nice surprise. Thank you so very much.

★ ★ ★

I guess you heard about the two women who were talking about a lady going down the street.

"Do you know her to speak to?" one asked the other.

"No, only to talk about."

This lovely gift will be something to talk about for a long, long time. Thank you so much.

★ ★ ★

From the bottom of my heart I wish to thank you for the kindness you have shown me today. It is very pleasant to receive such compliments. I will determine to be more worthy of your praise.

★ ★ ★

I accept this office with such a deep sense of pride. Pride in your confidence in me and pride in being able to serve such a great organization.

★ ★ ★

With a deep sense of humility I start my duties as your president today. I hold our organization in great esteem and will try my best to serve faithfully.

... Announcements of Things to Come

For all who desire to participate in the fun and fellowship of a fund raising party next Friday night at eight o'clock, we say welcome. The money raised will be used to buy books for our new church library.

★ ★ ★

Will you accept the challenge of the men of our church and attend the men's meeting in our Fellowship Hall next Tuesday evening. You will be inspired by the speaker, Rev. _____, from the city of _____.

★ ★ ★

On November 10th you will have the opportunity to hear one of the best-known speakers in our denomination. Come to City Hall at seven o'clock in the evening. There will be a small admission charge to cover the expenses of the speaker and the rent on the hall.

★ ★ ★

You will not want to miss a service of our series of revival services starting next Sunday. Come with deep humility and a deepening faith in God. We will want to make this a great event in our church.

★ ★ ★

All hands are needed at our spring picnic. Come, bring your basket lunch and your family. We will meet at the city park at six o'clock in the evening. There will be entertainment for all ages.

★ ★ ★

Many invitations will be sent to relatives and friends from out of town but for fear some will be missed we want all of you to have a personal invitation to attend the service of dedication for the new building named after Mr. and Mrs.

_____ who gave so generously to make the building possible.

The services will be held in front of the building at three o'clock next Sunday afternoon.

★   ★   ★

Take note of a director's meeting at 5:00 P.M. in the chapel.

★   ★   ★

We will start a Career Department in our Sunday School next Sunday morning. Mr. _____ will be the teacher. All young people who are in the career category are invited to meet in room _____ at 10:00 A.M.

★   ★   ★

We especially want all of you to be present from 2 to 5 P.M. Next Friday in the lower auditorium. At that time we will have two noted authors as our guests.

★   ★   ★

Our monthly fellowship dinner will be Wednesday night at 6:45 P.M. in Fellowship Hall. All members are asked to bring a dish or two of food.

. . . Words by a Young Man about to Be Ordained as a Minister

Some years ago, in answer to the call of God upon my life, I left my job and entered school to better prepare for service. I have sought to be faithful to my call for special service and enter every open door to give my testimony and proclaim God's saving power.

Now a wider door, as a pastor, has opened and I feel it will be an enlarged opportunity to answer God's call upon me to minister to the needs of people.

The Lord has dealt with me several months about accepting ordination in the ministry. God has revealed this to me to be His will. Now I am ready to make this step of faith. The openness and love with which many of the leaders of this church have received me has led me to believe this is a step in the direction God would have me go.

I have felt the mighty anointing of the Holy Spirit. Obstacles I felt I could not surmount have been removed by the grace of God.

First Corinthians 16:9, "For a great door and effectual is opened unto me. . . ."

I am glad God called me to preach and will try to serve my generation to the best of my ability.

Please keep me constantly in your prayers.

... Taking the Offering

Accept, we pray, our offerings today. Use them for the growth of thy kingdom. Help us to withhold nought of our goods, talents and time from thee.

★ ★ ★

We thank thee Father for all thy many blessings to us. Now we come to return a portion of our goods to Thee. When we need thee we can always call and our needs are supplied. Help us not to be small in our gifts to thee.

★ ★ ★

On this lovely Sabbath morning as we come into the presence of our Lord, we are eagerly awaiting the peace and comfort to sustain our soul. Bless us as we bring our offering for the carrying on of the Kingdom.

★ ★ ★

Father bless all who bring gifts to thee at this time. Knowing "It is more blessed to give than to receive," May our gifts be generous and given freely.

★ ★ ★

One minister was talking to another.
"Cal, do you use notes?"
"No sir! I used to use notes but now I demand the cash."
Folks we need a cash offering for this special need which has arisen in our church.

. . . Congratulations on Special Occasions

Congratulations on the honor your school has bestowed upon you. We believe it could not happen to a nicer person.

★　　★　　★

Congratulations on the lovely trip you are about to take. We hope you have a joyous and blessed holiday. We shall pray for your safety and good health while you are away.

★　　★　　★

We wish to congratulate you on your successful adoption of a beautiful baby. We felt honored that you used our name as a reference when filling out the forms. May this little one bring much happiness into your home, we pray.

★　　★　　★

You are to be congratulated on your graduation. We know how hard you have worked and dreamed to make this day a reality.

We have hope and confidence in your future and we know many of your dreams will come true.

★　　★　　★

So you are a graduate! Congratulations and best wishes. This is a season full of beauty for your life. We hope it brings to you a hope for greater and better things in the future. We love and appreciate you and the effort you have put forth to reach this day.

★　　★　　★

Congratulations on your twenty-fifth wedding anniversary. You are two wonderful people and the family you have brought up is a credit to our community. We hope this special day will indeed be special and you will live to enjoy many more years together.

★　　★　　★

I want to congratulate you both on fifty years of happy

married life. You have been of service to your church and your community. Your children are an honor to your name. It is wonderful that God has seen fit to spare you for these fifty years together. Our wish is that there will be many more and the showers of God's blessings will continue to fall upon you.

★　　★　　★

Congratulations upon your election to your new office. I count it a great privilege to know you. At times I have thought you were doing the work of several people. We are thankful that God has blessed your efforts with this new office.

★　　★　　★

Congratulations upon the unanimous and enthusiastic vote of approval by the deacon body upon your being recommended to the church as a new worker. We think you are the greatest and we are glad to have you around.

... Nomination of Someone for an Office

"Mr. Chairman, I nominate _____."

(Nominating speech.)

(Give qualifications of nominee. How he can best fill the requirements for the office.)

(Give some of the nominee's experience and training.)

(Mention some of the good points about his character; courage, wisdom, sense of justice, leadership ability.)

★　★　★

(Another type of nominating speech is to give many of the above qualifications but withhold the name until the last. This is not considered the best form of nomination.)

★　★　★

I have been impelled to nominate Mr. _____ because he has the qualifications I believe we need in this office. His wide experience in meeting the public will enable him to represent us without hesitation. He will preserve friendship for our organization with his friendly out-going personality. Yet he is a man of wisdom and demands the respect of all who know him.

If you see fit to elect Mr. _____ to this office I predict a greater future for our organization.

... Promotion of Christian Literature

Nobody knows, yes, and nobody cares
One thing about what an old woman wears;
    And so I just go around as I please,
    Hat awry and my mind all at ease.

But now and then, as my old spirits burn,
Velvets and laces to my fancy return.
    Decked out with earbobs and hair freshly curled,
    Out then I go with a smile for the world.

Yet still I'm passed by in the rush of the street.
And very few but my friends do I greet.
    Nobody knows, yes, and nobody cares
    What is the style that an old woman wears.

                    —Amy Bolding

The style show we are about to have today is not a show of the newest style in ladies' fashions. We are going to have a review of the latest style in what to read if you are a member of our Denomination.

(Start with the magazine you have for the youngest age group and let a young child bring one across the stage. Promote all your periodicals in this manner using the age person suitable for the magazine or paper.

For the State paper use the pastor or some other official in the church.

Close with a brief pep talk urging people to read the literature provided by the church.

It is well at the close to have all stand in a row holding their magazine facing the audience.)

. . . Scripture for Hospital and Sickbed Visitation

"God is our strength and refuge, a very present help in trouble. Be still and know that I am God." — Psalm 46

"Casting all your care upon him, for he careth for you."
I Peter 5:7

"Come unto me, all ye that are heavy laden, and I will give you rest." — Matthew 11:28

"The Lord is near to all who call upon him."

—Psalm 145:18

"Fear not for I am with you." — Isaiah 43:5

"What time I am afraid, I will put my trust in thee."

—Psalm 56:3

"Commit thy way unto the Lord; trust also in him; and he shall bring it to pass." — Psalm 37:5

. . . Pastor's Prayer at a Sickbed

Our dear, merciful, heavenly Father, we come to thee with burdened hearts for this dear child of thine. Look down upon him today and heal his body. We thank thee for good doctors and nurses but we ask thee to be the Great Physician and guide them as they minister to this precious child of thine. We thank thee for the blessings of the past and would ask for an abundant shower of healing blessings at this time. Hasten the recovery of this patient and restore him again to his family and home. Amen.

... Prayer with Family during Surgery

Our Father, we know thou art with us at this time. As our hearts are burdened with worry and care help us to trust all to thy love and care. Guide the surgeon's hands, give him just the skill he needs for this delicate operation. We thank thee for the blessing of healing we know thou wilt grant to _____. Amen.

★　★　★

"Happy shalt thou be, and it shall be well with thee."

—Psalm 128:2

God's way is the best way,
    Though I may not see
Why sorrows and trials
    Oft gather 'round me.
He ever is seeking
    My gold to refine,
I'll trust in Him always,
    My Saviour divine.

. . . Talking with a Sick Child

We are so sorry you are ill but the good doctors and nurses will do their best to make you well again.

Do you remember the story and picture of Christ as he carried the little, lost lamb back to the fold? Today He is very near you and will hold you tightly in His arms until you are well again. His loving hands along with those of your mother and father will comfort and keep you.

(Quote the 23rd Psalm.)

★　　★　　★

Let us today remember the verse in Romans 8:28. "And we know that all things work together for good to them that love God, to them who are called according to his purpose."

Have faith today in the one who made the promise we just quoted. He has power to relieve the pain, to heal the body. Jesus said, "All power is given to me in Heaven and on earth," so trust His power to make you well.

Wisdom from Wise Men

Ultimate freedom is your right to choose your own attitude.

★   ★   ★

"Nations may be through with God but God is not through with them."— Marshall Craig

★   ★   ★

Some teaching is merely the exchange of ignorance.

★   ★   ★

"It is one thing to have a well-ordered philosophy, another to practice the will of God." — Roy McClung

★   ★   ★

"I can't preach but I sure do love Jesus." — E. Stanley Jones

★   ★   ★

Knowledge humbleth the great man, astonisheth the common man, and puffeth up the little man.

★   ★   ★

If you want pure silver you must put it in the fire, keep putting it in the fire and trying it until you can see your face in it, then take it out. So God must see his face reflected in us.

★   ★   ★

Ill fares the land, to hastening
ills a prey,
Where wealth accumulates, and
men decay.
—Oliver Goldsmith

★   ★   ★

People sometimes make monkeys out of themselves by carrying tales.

★   ★   ★

"Cheerfulness and contentment are great beautifiers and are famous preservers of youthful looks." — Charles Dickens.

★   ★   ★

Happiness is a perfume you cannot pour on others without spilling a few drops on yourself.

★　　★　　★

To have faith is to create;
To have hope is to call down blessing;
To have love is to work miracles.
　　　　　　　　　　　—Michael Fairless

★　　★　　★

No one ever graduates from Bible Study until he meets its author face to face.

★　　★　　★

The church is the home's greatest ally. It is the parent's truest friend. Your child needs a sense of security in a transient world. In the church and its message there is a sense of that fixedness, steadfastness, and security which is essential to well being. — J. Howard Williams

★　　★　　★

A man becomes wise by watching what happens to him when he isn't.

★　　★　　★

"In prayer it is better to have a heart without words than words without heart." — John Bunyan

★　　★　　★

"There is a vast difference between praying prayers and saying prayers." — Frances Taylor

★　　★　　★

Forbidden fruit is responsible for many a bad jam.

★　　★　　★

When right you can afford to keep your temper;
When wrong you can't afford to lose it.

★　　★　　★

He that winneth souls is wise.

★　　★　　★

Many a church member would be scared to death, if he

could only feel his spiritual pulse and find out how nearly dead he is.

★   ★   ★

There are no permanent residents on Easy Street.

★   ★   ★

Real justice is given when judge and jury give the same verdict God would give.

★   ★   ★

You may be on the right track, which is good, but if you just sit there you will get run over, which is bad.

★   ★   ★

Gossip is a negative which should never be enlarged and developed.

★   ★   ★

Be sure your young man is not burning all his midnight oil in a crankcase.

★   ★   ★

The happiest business in the world is that of making friends.

★   ★   ★

"The greatest thing in this world is not so much where we are going, but in what direction we are moving." — Holmes

★   ★   ★

I had learned that one cannot tremble and trust at the same time, and I dared not go without trusting.

★   ★   ★

"Without Christ, life is a hopeless end, but with Christ life is an endless hope." — James Robison

★   ★   ★

Some people look as if they had been vaccinated on pickle juice.

★   ★   ★

"The greatest friend of the church is persecution. The greatest enemy of the church is prosperity." — Robison

★   ★   ★

"Shed no tears over your lack of early advantages. No

really great man ever had any advantages that he himself did not create." — Elbert Hubbard

★ ★ ★

"I do not remember a single case of a boy or girl who attended Sunday School regularly being brought into court."
—Judge Sarah T. Hughes

★ ★ ★

Real love is like the sunshine. Even when it is behind a cloud you know it is still there.

★ ★ ★

"I come here to find myself. It is so easy to get lost in the world." — Printed on Bok Tower in Florida

★ ★ ★

The battlefield of life is littered with the remains of men who knew too much and believed too little.

★ ★ ★

"Let not him who is homeless pull down the house of another, but let him labor diligently to build one for himself." — Lincoln

★ ★ ★

There is nothing so certain as uncertainty.

★ ★ ★

"One thorn of experience is worth a whole wilderness of warning." — Lowell

★ ★ ★

"It is not work that kills men; it is worry. Work is healthy; you can hardly put more upon a man that he can bear. Worry is rust upon the blade. It is not the revolution that destroys the machinery, but the friction." — Henry Ward Beecher

★ ★ ★

"You can't say civilization doesn't advance however, for in every war they kill you a new way." — Will Rogers

★ ★ ★

There's room at the top and you get a better view.

★　★　★

Seek gold by digging.

★　★　★

Plant the tap root of your faith in deep soil.

★　★　★

"You will never make your mark unless you stand alone."

—Patience Strong

★　★　★

A man can wait patiently, especially if he thinks he is going to get some money out of it.

★　★　★

Playing second fiddle does not always make for harmony.

★　★　★

For good health we should supplement proper diet with faith and clean living.

★　★　★

Success is never permanent. And fortunately, neither is failure.

★　★　★

Any little man can criticize. It takes a big man to sympathize. Measure yourself!

★　★　★

A fool dreams of wealth, a wise man of happiness.

★　★　★

A wise man remembers his friends at all times; a fool, only when he has need of them.

★　★　★

He who speaks evil to you of others will speak evil of you to others.

★　★　★

"Be sure you put your feet in the right place and then stand firm." — Lincoln.

★　★　★

A person may overcome his lack of beauty by living a beautiful life.

★　★　★

Never use tones that crush and words that bite, study the language of gentleness.

★　★　★

Men are born with two eyes but with one tongue in order that they should see twice as much as they say.

★　★　★

Unlike the poet, the successful man is not born.

★　★　★

For a lost traveler along the road, it is far better to find a road sign, even in stark simplicity, than a painting by Picasso.

★　★　★

Our pride, our selfishness, all show that we do not understand that we were made to serve, not to be served.

★　★　★

Life is not so short but that there is always time for courtesy.

★　★　★

If you use the heart with which you forgive yourself to forgive others, there will be perfect friendship.

★　★　★

A blessed life is the fruit of the present, and eternal life is the hope of the future.

★　★　★

The man who loves his neighbor as himself, soon discovers God has moved into his neighborhood.

★　★　★

This is success—to be able to carry money without spending it; to be able to hear an injustice without retaliating; to be able to do one's duty even when one is not watched; to be able to keep at the job until it is finished; to be able to make use of criticism without letting it whip you.